DATING SECRETS FOR THE INTROVERTS

Discover How to Eliminate Dating Fear, Anxiety and Shyness by Instantly Raising Your Charm and Confidence with These Simple Techniques.

By
James W. Williams

Copyright © 2018
All rights reserved.

No part of this publication may be copied, reproduced in any format, by any means, electronic or otherwise, without prior consent from the copyright owner and publisher of this book.

Table Of Contents

INTRODUCTION 5

DRESS THE PART 7

GET OUT OF THE HOUSE 12

STEP OUT OF YOUR COMFORT ZONE........... 18

TAKE THE INITIATIVE 23

KEEP THE CONVERSATION GOING 28

CLOSING.. 33

Thank you! 35

Your Free Gift

As a way of saying thanks for your purchase, I wanted to offer you a free bonus E-book called *"Bulletproof Confidence Checklist: Eliminate Limiting Beliefs, Overcome Shyness and Social Anxiety and Achieve Your Goals"*.

In this guide, you will discover:

- What is shyness & social anxiety and the psychology behind it
- Simple treatments for social anxiety
- Breakdown of the traits of a confident person
- Breakdown of the traits of a socially awkward person
- Easy, actionable tips for overcoming being socially awkward
- Confidence checklist to ensure you're on the right path of self-development

To grab your free bonus book just tap here, or go to:

https://theartofmastery.com/confidence/

INTRODUCTION

If you have accepted the social tag "introvert", congratulations! You fall into the elusive category of one of the most sought-after men in today's dating game. Of course, you may not be feeling very sought-after right this minute. At the end of this introduction, you might realize that you may have missed out on more opportunities with the ladies than you know because you weren't paying attention. First, let us answer the impertinent question of why introverts are ranking higher on most women's "hot list".

Introverts have this general air of mystery to them and mystery in a man is woman magnet. Add this to that highly sensitive nature that characterizes most introverts (think Ryan Gosling in the movie, Drive), you create an irresistible aura. There is also statistics supporting the theory that introverts are less likely to cheat than their more outgoing peers. Put all of these together in one person aka you and it is not hard to understand why you have become the ideal mate.

So, if you really are that much of a big deal, how come numbers (or ladies) are not falling on your lap? Because you are meant to lead in a relationship. This is not bigotry, it is just the way of things. If you tend to get asked out a lot by the ladies, you will discover a disturbing pattern in your relationships. It is either you find yourself settling for less than you deserve, or you are at the whims of someone controlling.

It is possible to be true to who you are and still take an active lead role in your relationship. Sometimes, all you need is the green light. Not every woman has that direct I-want-you-to-ask-me-out gaze but here are a few things that might indicate the lady (or ladies) are interested.

1. You make eye contact from across the room a lot and there is a spark every time you lock gaze.

2. She genuinely enjoys talking to you

3. Her arms are relaxed or wide open when she is talking to you

4. She hints at plans for the future that involve you

5. She is following you online and actively likes or comments on your posts

CHAPTER ONE

DRESS THE PART

The main tool required for opening conversations with women is confidence. A guy may have no exceptional body features and even look like he got dressed in the dark but with plenty of confidence, he can charm the most stunning woman in the room and walk out leaving said woman (among others) hanging on his every word as if her life depends on it. Not everyone is born with that level of confidence. However, everyone can grow their confidence level to enable them to initiate that one conversation that could change their lives forever.

The basic confidence builder is appearance. Granted, we cannot all look like Tom Cruise physically or have enough money to fund a cosmetic transformation (I wouldn't recommend it anyway). So, beyond visiting the gym to whip yourself into shape, there isn't much you can do about your physical appearance. You can, however, play up your appearance with clothes. With a little guidance and careful investment in your closet, you can infuse your style sense with your personality and show the world who you are.

There is a general saying that applies to life and to dating as well. Stylists and fashion gurus are quick to dispense the phrase "dress to impress" to eager fashionistas and while it may be applicable in certain context, in the dating game, it can prove to be fatal. This is because it is only possible to impress someone you know or in the very least have an idea of what their likes and preferences are. In your case, you have not even met or started dating yet, so how can you truly impress her?

My advice is dress for you. Wear what makes you feel confident. Get well fitting clothes. Choose colors that work well with your skin tone (yes, there is such a thing). Wear patterns that don't make you look overwhelmed and avoid clothes that make you nervous and fidgety (because you are not comfortable). It is unattractive and throws your confidence off balance. The best fashion advice I ever got was from my father. Always dress like the best version of you. In other words, dress to impress you.

A lot of introverts like to dress for comfort and while this is applaudable, this "comfort" dressing tends to morph into a casual homeless look that does not really communicate who you are underneath all those layers (or lack of) of fabric. Again, I am not asking you to dress like you just stepped out of a page of a GQ magazine (although that has its perks). All I am saying is that you pay attention to your clothes. Before you throw up your hands in despair, I took the liberty of including some fashion pointers to help you get started on your new fashion journey. They are simple but if applied, could make a significant impact in your style.

1. Press your shirts

It is amazing the difference putting iron on your clothes could make versus when you wear them with wrinkles and all. It doesn't matter if the shirt spots a designer label or not. Wrinkles on your clothes makes you appear careless, cheap and certainly not date worthy. Ironed clothes on the other hand gives you a sharp and distinguished look even if it is just jeans and t-shirt.

2. Pair patterns and colors cautiously

Using certain colors together have a clownish effect and while everyone may like the clown, not many women are eager to go home with one. Don't get me wrong. Women love guys that make them laugh. But nothing can shrink your confidence faster that finding out that she is laughing at you rather than with you. As a general rule, try not to wear more than 3 predominant colors in one outfit.

3. Know what clothes are appropriate

Showing up at a black-tie event in jeans and biker boots might excite the rebel in you but it is also a one-way track to becoming isolated at events that is if you ever get invited at all. Sure, you want to express your personal style in your outfit but, it is important that you know what belongs where.

Besides, with accessories, you can add that personal touch that stands you out without making you the odd ball.

Unless your fashion journey involves professional stylists, it may take a while to wear you in the fashion sense. You may have some trial and error experiences along the way but with each attempt, you gain more confidence. Beyond boosting your confidence, dressing well creates a good impression of you which is essential when you meet new people. It may sound unfair, but your dressing helps formulate people's opinion of you. So, don't be afraid to begin this process. It is time to show the world the sophisticated and more confident you.

CHAPTER TWO

GET OUT OF THE HOUSE

For an introvert, dating might involve you doing the exact opposite of what you love to do which is meeting people. This might be a daunting experience for even the bravest of men but, you have to start from somewhere. As you make a foray into the social scene, it is important you pay attention to your scenes carefully. Brazenly walking into a hot night spot might be akin to ripping the bandages off but the "sensory" overload can have some serious backlash resulting in the decision to "never again". My recommendation? Baby steps.

Start by visiting places that interests you. If you are an art lover for instance, places like the museum and gallery could provide a more positive experience. That is because, it holds things or events that appeal to you. Also, in these kinds of settings, you might run into people who share similar interests. People with similar interests mean you have more to talk about and when you have more to talk about, you give yourself and your prospective date a chance to really get to know each other. If nothing else, at least, you get to indulge in something that you actually like.

Choose places you are familiar with. For the proper introvert, there is no familiar place like home. And with Netflix and chill as legitimate dating options, we don't necessarily see the need to go out. It would be kind of me to point out here that the Netflix and chill date only happens when you have an actual date. Unless dates have started falling out of the sky and straight into your living room, you will have to go out. But, it doesn't have to be too far from home. Your favorite coffee shop could be a good spot. You are familiar with the waiters; the menu and this kind of familiarity might make you less self-conscious. The less awkward things are, the better your chances of scoring her number (and possibly a date if you put your best foot forward).

Go out in packs. Ever been to a bar or a party and seen that weird guy in the corner casting weary glances across the room and giving out awkward body language in his poor attempt to strike a conversation? Chances are you have been that guy. It can be hard to pitch a lady when you have that sad cloud hanging over you. Having a social pack can help you feel as part of the group without having to do anything beyond being there. This gives you a chance to scope the room for prospective dates and zero in on your interest. Plus, if your buddies are the outgoing type, they could get that initial awkward conversation out of the way and help you enjoy your time out.

I am going to skip ahead here and take you to a possible scenario where you have been set up on a blind date. There are a lot of mixed feelings when it comes to blind dates. For starters, it could be a relief to have someone else set you up. All you must do is dress up, show up and hope to God it works. On the other hand, it can feel awkward. Like how you are at lunch with your best bud and then this other girl shows up and then your friend suddenly has to "attend to an emergency". Painfully awkward. I would vote for the former. If you are lucky enough to have friends who set you up with the ladies, please accept. It may not lead to "the relationship" right away but, it gives you the chance to practice.

HOW TO SURVIVE A BLIND DATE

1. Try and get a little information about your date. People who meet through online dating platforms have more leverage in this regard as you spend the pre-date period chatting to get to know each other.

2. Choose somewhere where you will both be at ease.

3. Plan to keep things short and sweet. Not all dates turn out to be great. Plan on something that would not prolong the agony if you end up in date hell.

4. Don't shy away from unconventional dates. Be open to trying something different. Just be sure to give your date the heads-up too.

An interesting date option for me during my early dating years was choosing an activity instead of a place. Traditional dating requires people sitting at a table over a meal and talking to get to know each other. Typically, I am quite comfortable doing the listening while the lady does the talking but after a while, most ladies assume you either don't have an interesting life or you are just not interested in sharing. So, I decided to show my personality instead of just telling her about it. Sailing was something me and my buddies did every other weekend. And so, for a date, I invited Sara on a boating trip.

I had 3 of my closest friends and their girlfriends over. It was a crowdy scene but, Sarah got to see me in my element in the company of the people I am most comfortable with in the whole world. It was my comfort zone and featured activities (apart from eating) that I was interested in.

Barring the ear-piercing scream Sara let out when she caught a fish, I would say that was my most successful first date ever. By combining all the elements of a great first date; comfort, familiarity and great company, I was able to get over the awkward first huddle and actually enjoy getting to know someone.

CHAPTER THREE

STEP OUT OF YOUR COMFORT ZONE

After all the grief I gave you in the previous chapter about staying with the familiar and sticking with what you are comfortable with, I can understand your confusion here but, stay with me. I am taking you somewhere. In the beginning, I talked about taking baby steps. You don't wake up one day a baby who can barely flip over on their stomach and then the next day you are running down a flight of stairs. It starts with carefully learning to coordinate your muscles, gain mastery over them, having a few practice tryouts and before you finally take a plunge.

In this case, first, you work on boosting your confidence by paying attention to your appearance. Then, you start going out to familiar places. After that, you explore a bit more. To improve your dating prospects, you need to widen your search pool. Social dating apps are great as they connect you with people you probably would never have met otherwise but, it also has the great disadvantage of keeping you confined to your comfort zone. You need to go out there and really experience life even if that may sometimes mean sharing that experience with other people. Being an introvert, I understand how you would prefer our own company to anyone else' but if you are going to date, you are going to start liking the company of other people too.

Now that we have established this, here are a few additional benefits of stepping out of your comfort zones

1. You get to know yourself better.

Trying out new things puts you in a position to test your limits. How can you tell you are not going to like Indian cuisine if you have never really tried it? Life is happening outside the walls of your room and going out there is one of the best ways to live it. The flip side of the coin is that by stepping out of your area of comfort, you get to discover if your introversive nature is linked to social anxiety or if it is even more deep rooted than that. Whatever the case, each new experience reveals a new layer of you.

2. It enriches your life.

There is no question about it. Not all is good and right in the world and there is a 50% chance that your quest to find a date could be a horrific experience ranging anywhere from mild drama at the table to psycho date from hell. But, in the kaleidoscope of life, the good and the bad adds more "flavor" to your experiences and makes you better for it. Imagine the stories you would share with the grand kids (if you are into that sort of thing).

3. It improves your confidence.

Trying out something new for the first time whether is an activity, visiting a new place or meeting new people, is a daunting task. But, it is an excellent confidence builder. It is kind of ironic when you think about it. That in facing your fears, you overcome them and with each victory, you become bolder and more confident. The psychology behind it is that in facing your fears, your find your strengths. Look it this way, to build muscle mass with workouts, you need to push your muscles past that comfort zone. In the same way, to bulk up your confidence muscle, you have to try something new.

4. You might actually enjoy it!

This is a no brainer. The moment you get past the mental barriers such as fear and anxiety, you might be surprised by how much you enjoy it. Hanging out with the boys after work may (in the most positive way) prove to be a more fulfilling experience than the crew from that Comedy Central show who keep you company every week night on the couch. And if not, there is always that record button. It always comes in handy.

So, we know that stepping out of your comfort zone has these fantastic benefits but what does it really have to do with dating? We started this journey with a purpose. To whip out your charm and raise your confidence to the optimum date maestro levels. Remember that ship and harbor quote? A ship at harbor is safe but that is not what ships are meant for. You are not meant to sit back on your couch night after night hoping that you miraculously run into your soul mate on your way to the washroom. Try out at least one new activity every day and in the spirit of taking baby steps, I made a list of simple tasks you can start with. Be sure to add to the list and keep at it daily.

- Try a new coffee flavor at your favorite cafe
- Maintain a 2 second eye contact at a perfect stranger and smile at them
- Compliment the first girl you see in the morning (your dog or cat does not count)
- In your outfit of the day, include one brightly colored item
- Push your curfew time by one hour

CHAPTER FOUR

TAKE THE INITIATIVE

This is the part where a lot of introverts lose their nerves. They work up the courage, boost their confidence levels only to become tongue tied at the point of communication or completely abandon ship altogether. But that is not going to happen with you because you have me. And that is saying a lot! Let us demystify this cloud that hangs over the task of asking out a beautiful woman. We will start by getting the worst out of the way. You dread her response. But here is the only thing that can happen, she would either say yes or no.

I have never heard of someone who got smacked in the head for trying to scoop a pretty woman. Well, unless you were rude and obnoxious, or a husband or boyfriend happened to be close by and in that case, you should politely tell him you were just paying her a compliment, then back off and move on to a woman who is available. But, let's not debate scenarios because that is how you lose your courage in the first place. Instead, let us look at the two most likely responses you would get. Anything else would fall in the less than 10% category.

Nothing deflates one's ego faster than the word "No". Well, I can think of a few things but, let us keep things sanitary here. You have done the work, put in some really good effort into your appearance, visited the familiar and unfamiliar and now that you are feeling confident, you walk up to your dream girl and she just turns you down. It doesn't matter if she said a few nice things to soften the blow (well, it helps), it still hurts anyway. But here is the real deal, this is the worst that could happen.

If everyone threw in the towel every time they heard the word "no", many of us wouldn't have been born. You should not give up. There is a twisted version this advice I just gave you were guys are encouraged to keep pressurizing the said girl until she caves in and says yes. That is just creepy and wrong in every sense of the word. When I say you shouldn't give up, I meant don't stop trying to find your dream girl. She is out there. Because, one of the most defining qualities of your dream girl is that she thinks you are her dream guy. You deserve nothing less. So, if you enter into the dating game with this mindset, you would understand that no simply means, she doesn't see her mate in you ergo, she is not the one.

Admittedly, it is a downer, but you shouldn't stay down. Be okay with it and don't take it as a personal affront. However, if you pay attention and play your cards right, there are certain things you can do to improve your chances of getting a yes.

1. Before you make your move, you can actually tell if she is into you or not. I talked about this in the introduction. Subtle nuances and body language can indicate interest. Of course, this is not 100% foolproof but, it helps.

2. Don't try to be cocky or over confident. It is okay to fake it in certain situations but not this one. Ladies can smell a phony for miles. Be yourself and you would find that those clumsy gestures and stuttering might be a redeeming quality. I know you would rather do it without the awkwardness but if this is who you are own it.

3. Choose your words carefully. A lot of times, those pickup lines your read about in dating books could leave you falling flat on your face. There are conversation starters you could use to break the ice. They don't have to be lewd or suggestive just genuine.

4. Do a quick check or have your buddies do it for you before you make your movie. Look sharp and make sure that there are no lingering evidences of your salad in your mouth. And most importantly, check that there you are not wearing the all-natural "eww de cologne". It is difficult for a lady to say yes to bad breath and body odor.

In the next likely event where this magical lady says yes to you, all I can say is congratulations!

You have found a special woman. But, your work is far from done. In the next chapter, we explore ideas for your first date, navigating first date hurdles and provide practical tips on how to keep the conversation flowing.

CHAPTER FIVE

KEEP THE CONVERSATION GOING

Right after asking a girl out, the next panic inducing problem is what to do on your first date. You want everything to play out perfectly like a montage from those romantic chic flicks. Unless you are in an actual movie or you have the event planner for the British royalty on speed dial, you can kiss the perfect date goodbye. That is not to say you should expect Murphy's law to take effect either. I am just saying that you shouldn't sweat the small stuff so much that you break out in a rash. Sure, you want to make sure that she has a great time. That is noble, and your heart is in the right place. But, you should also make sure you are having a great time too. If both of you are enjoying yourselves, the date qualifies as a success and you can go on to making other plans.

Traditionally, most people like sit downs at restaurants. Or picnics in interesting places.

These days, people have come up with more unconventional ideas. From hiking popular trails to visiting famous landmarks. Unless this is someone who runs in the same social circle as you, you may need help in sorting this one out. In the time that you have secured your date, I am almost certain that you secured her number too. The straight forward approach would be to ring or chat her up and ask her plainly if she has any ideas for where she might want to go. If you are lucky, she may have a specific place in mind. The problem with this kind of approach is that you have a 50% chance of her suggesting somewhere above budget or a place with bad memories for you. You can either agree to it or recommend somewhere similar based on her preference.

The romantics would prefer a different approach. You want to figure out your lady and sweep her off her feet with grand gestures. That is all great, just be sure that you don't get swept out the door for your efforts. The key is to be genuine and remain true to yourself in all that you do. You are still getting to know this person. Figuring them out is part of a process that takes more time that a first date would permit. Let the unraveling of each other be in the experiences that bonds you guys together.

No matter what route you chose, the one thing that matters is that you show up and show up on time. It is rude and unacceptable to keep your date waiting. If she starts acting out even before the starters arrive, I can't say I blame her. I have fumed at clients who treated me with less respect. You could offer to pick her up to avoid this. And if you find that you are running late even by 1 minute, pick up your phone and call her. This way, she knows that she is important to you and she doesn't feel disrespected.

With the whole feminist movement, it is hard to tell if your chivalrous gestures might be interpreted as insulting or caring. I would say, be who you are. If you naturally chivalrous, by all means be chivalrous. Whatever the case, be at your best behavior. Stand when she stands and sit after she is seated. Pull out her chair if that is your thing (I personally think every guy should make it their thing). And most importantly be attentive.

The next part is starting a conversation and keeping it going. The general rule of keeping conversations is asking open ended questions. These are questions that require more than a yes or no response. But in asking your questions, try not to let things segue into an interrogation at a job interview. Keep the questions light, interesting and please try not to be a critic. That is like third date move. The subject of religion, political affiliations and sordid pasts should be left for subsequent dates. You can talk about interests, passions and anything else that bring the spark to both your eyes. Be a good conversationalist. Give as good as you are getting.

Keeping date conversation going is a very delicate balance between body language and use of words. This may sound like plenty work. But if you relax and try to have a good time, the rest would come to you naturally.

CLOSING

Love is a beautiful thing and when you find the right person for you, it is worth every social hurdle you had to overcome to be with this person. From experience, I can tell you that those things you are afraid of are more often than not in your head than a reality. You have created these mental barriers that keep you from living the life you are meant to live. You deserve to be happy, but you must make up your mind to create your own happiness even if it means doing the things that scare you the most. The pluses far outweigh the cost and your life would be richer for it.

Use each day to learn new things about you. Open yourself a little more. Smile more. And don't assume that everyone out there is judging you for who they are. And even if they are judging, you know that their opinions don't count so why would want to live your life for them anyway.

Commit to living each day in the most authentic version of yourself. Because, it is when we are truly who we are that we find strength, confidence and love. Remember, you deserve the best.

James W. Williams

Thank you!

Before you go, I just wanted to say thank you for purchasing my book.

You could have picked from dozens of other books on the same topic but you took a chance and chose this one.

So, a HUGE thanks to you for getting this book and for reading all the way to the end.

Now I wanted to ask you for a small favor. **Could you please consider posting a review on the platform? Reviews are one of the easiest ways to support the work of independent authors.**

This feedback will help me continue to write the type of books that will help you get the results you want. So if you enjoyed it, please let me know! (-:

Lastly, don't forget to grab a copy of your Free Bonus book *"Bulletproof Confidence Checklist"*. If you want to learn how to overcome shyness and social anxiety and become more confident then this book is for you.

Just go to
https://theartofmastery.com/confidence/

www.ingramcontent.com/pod-product-compliance
Lightning Source LLC
Chambersburg PA
CBHW060034040426
42333CB00042B/2448